Carl Jung
Face to Face

ERIS
gems

SWITZERLAND. CARL GUSTAV JUNG. *Born in 1875. With Freud, one of the founding fathers of modern psychology. Still working at eighty-four, he is the most honored living psychiatrist, and history will record him as one of the greatest physicians of all time. How many years have you lived in this lovely house by the lake at Zurich?*

It's just about fifty years.

Do you live here now just with your secretaries and your English housekeeper?

Yes.

No children or grandchildren with you?

No, they don't live here, but I have plenty of them in the surroundings.

Do they come to see you often?

Oh, yes.

How many grandchildren do you have?

Oh, nineteen.

And great-grandchildren?

Oh, I think eight, and I suppose one is on the way.

And do you enjoy having them?

Well, of course it's nice to feel such a living

crowd out of oneself.

Are they afraid of you, do you think?

I don't think so. If you would know my grandchildren, you wouldn't think so. They steal my things. Even my hat that belongs to me they stole the other day.

Now, can I take you back to your own childhood? Do you remember the occasion when you first felt consciousness of your own individual self?

That was in my eleventh year. There I suddenly, on my way to school, I stepped out of a mist. It was just as if I had been in a mist, walking in a mist, and I stepped out of it, and I knew *I am*. I am what I am. And then I thought, "But what have I been before?" And then I found that I had been in a mist, not knowing to differentiate myself from things. I was just one thing among many.

Now, was that associated with any particular episode in your life, or was it just a normal function of adolescence?

Well, that's difficult to say. As far as I can

remember, nothing had happened before that would explain this sudden coming to consciousness.

You hadn't, for instance, been quarreling with your parents or anything?

No, no.

What memories have you of your parents? Were they strict and old-fashioned in the way they brought you up?

Oh well, you know, they belonged to the later parts of the Middle Ages, and my father was a person from the country, and you can imagine what people were then—you know, in the '70s of the past century. They had the convictions in which people have lived since 1,800 years.

How did he try to impress these convictions on you? Did he punish you for instance?

Oh no, not at all. No, he was very liberal and he was most tolerant, most understanding.

Which one is one always more intimately with—your father or your mother?

That's difficult to say. Of course, one is

always more intimate with the mother, but when it comes to the personal feeling I had a better relation to my father who was predictable, than with my mother who was to me a very problematic something.

So, at any rate, fear was not an element in your relation with your father?

Not at all.

Did you accept him as being infallible in his judgments?

Oh, no, I knew he was very fallible.

How old were you when you knew that?

Now, let me see. Perhaps eleven or twelve years old. It was together with the fact that I knew I was. And from then on, I saw that my father was different.

So the moment of self-revelation was closely connected with realizing the fallibility of your parents?

Yes, one could say so. But I realized that I had fear of my mother, but not during the day. There she was quite known to me, unpredictable, but in the night I had fear of my mother.

And can you remember why?

I have not the slightest idea why.

What about your school days? Were you happy at school?

In the beginning I was very happy to have companions, you know, because before I had been very lonely. We lived in the country. And I had no brother and no sister. My sister was born very much later, when I was nine years old. And so I was used to being alone, but I missed it. I missed company. And in school, it was wonderful to have company. But soon, you know, in a country school, naturally, I was far ahead. And then I began to be bored.

What sort of religious upbringing did your father give you?

Oh, we were Swiss Reformed.

And did he make you attend church regularly?

Oh, well, that was quite natural. Everybody went to church on Sunday.

And did you believe in God?

Oh, yes.

Do you now believe in God?

Now? Difficult to answer. I know. I don't need to believe. I know.

Well now, turning to the next staging point in your life, what made you decide to become a doctor?

That was in the first place a merely opportunistic choice. I really, originally, wanted to be an archaeologist: Assyriology, Egyptology, or something of the sort. I hadn't the money. The study was too expensive. So my second love then belonged to nature, particularly zoology. When I began my studies, I inscribed in the so-called philosophical faculty—that means, natural sciences. But then I soon saw that the career that was before me would make a schoolmaster of me. I never thought I had any chance to get any further because we had no money at all. And then I saw that that didn't suit my expectations, you know, I didn't want to become a schoolmaster. Teaching was just not what I was looking for. And so I remembered that my grandfather had been a doctor, and I knew that when I was studying medicine, I had a chance to study natural science—and to become a doctor, and a doctor can develop, you see. He can have a practice, he can choose his scientific interests, more or less. I would have more chance than being a schoolmaster. Also, the idea of doing something useful with human beings appealed to me.

And did you, when you decided to become a doctor, have difficulty in getting the training at school and in passing the exams?

I particularly had difficulty with certain teachers that didn't believe that I could write a decent thesis. I remember one case where the teacher had the habit to discuss the papers written by the pupils, and he took the best first. He went through the whole number of pupils, and I didn't appear; and I was badly troubled over it. And I thought, Well, it is impossible that my thesis can be that bad. And when he had finished, he said, "There is still one paper left over, and that is the one by Jung." He went on to say, "That would be by far the best paper if it hadn't been copied. He has just copied it somewhere; stolen. You are a thief, Jung. And if I knew where you had stolen it, I would fling you out of school." And I got mad, and I said, "This is the one thesis where I have worked the most, because the theme was interesting, in contradistinction to other themes which are not at all interesting to me." And then he said, "You are a liar. And if you can't prove that you haven't stolen that thing somewhere, then you get out of school."

Now, that was a very serious thing to me, because what else then, you see? And I hated that fellow. And that was the only man I could have killed, you know. If I had met him once at a dark corner, I would have shown him something of what I could do.

Did you often have violent thoughts about people when you were young?

No, not exactly; only when I got mad, well then I beat them up.

Did you often get mad?

Not so often, but then for good.

You were very strong and big, I imagine.

Yes, I was pretty strong and, you know, reared in the country with those peasant boys; it was a rough kind of life. And I would have been capable of violence, I know. I was a bit afraid of it. So I rather tried to avoid critical situations because I didn't trust myself. Once I was attacked by about seven boys. And I got mad. And I took one and just swung him around with his legs, you know, and beat down four of them. And then they were satisfied.

And were there any consequences from that afterwards?

Oh, I should say, yes. From then on, I was always suspected that I was at the bottom of every trouble. I was not, but they were afraid, and I was never attacked again.

Well now, when the time came that you qualified as a doctor, what made you decide to specialize in being an alienist?

That is rather an interesting point. When
I had finished my studies practically and
when I didn't know what I really wanted
to do, I had a big chance to follow one of
my professors. He was called to a new po-
sition in Munich, and he wanted me as
his assistant. But then, in that moment, I
studied for my final examination. I came
across the textbook, a textbook of psychiatry. Up to then, I thought nothing about
it because our professor then wasn't particularly interested. And I only read the
introduction to that book, where certain
things were said about maladjustment of
personality. That hit the nail on the head.
In that moment, I saw I must become an
alienist. My heart was thumping wildly in
that moment. And when I told my professor I wouldn't follow him, I would study
psychiatry, he couldn't understand it, nor
[did] my friends, because in those days
psychiatry was nothing, nothing at all.
But I saw a great chance to unite certain

contrasting things in myself—namely, besides medicine, besides natural science, I always had studied history of philosophy and such subjects. It was just as if suddenly two streams were joining.

And how long was it after you took that decision that you first came into contact with Freud?

Oh, you know, that was at the end of my studies, and then it took quite a while until I met Freud. You see, I finished my studies in 1900, and I met Freud only very much later. I read—well, in 1900, I already read his dream interpretation and Freud's studies about hysteria. But that was merely literary, you know, and then in 1907 I became acquainted with him personally.

Will you tell me how that happened? Did you go to Vienna?

Oh, well, I'd written a book about the psychology of dementia—called *Schizophrenia Then*. And I sent him that book and thus we became acquainted. I went to Vienna for a fortnight then and then we had very long and penetrating conversations; and that settled it.

And this long and penetrating conversation was followed by personal friendship?

Oh yes, it soon developed into a personal friendship.

And what sort of man was Freud?

Well he was a complicated nature, you know. I liked him very much, but I soon discovered that when he had thought something, then it was settled. While I was doubting all along the line. And it was impossible to discuss something *à fond*. You know, he had no philosophical education. Particularly, you see, I was studying Kant. And I was steeped in it. And that was far from Freud. So from the very beginning, there was a discrepancy.

Did you in fact grow apart later, partly because of a difference in temperamental approach to experiment and proof and so on?

Well, of course, there is always a temperamental difference. And his approach was naturally different from mine because his personality was different from mine. That led me into my later investigation of psychological types. There are definite attitudes. Some people are doing it in this way and other people are doing it in a typical way. And there were such differences between myself and Freud, too.

Do you consider that Freud's standard of proof and experimentation was less high than your own?

Well, you see, that is an evaluation I am not competent to make. I am not my own history or my historiographer. With reference to certain results, I think my method has its merits.

Tell me, did Freud himself ever analyze you?

Oh yes, I submitted quite a lot of my dreams to him, and so did he.

And he to you, yes?

Oh yes, yes.

Do you remember now at this distance of time what were the significant features of Freud's dreams that you noted at the time?

Well, that is rather indiscreet to ask. You know there is such a thing as a professional secret.

He's been dead these many years.

Yes, but these regards last longer than life. I prefer not to talk about it.

Well, may I ask you something else, then, which perhaps is also indiscreet? Is it true that you have a very large number of letters which you exchanged with Freud which are still unpublished?

Yes.

When are they going to be published?

Well, not during my lifetime.

You would have no objection to them being published after your lifetime?

Oh, no, not at all.

Because they are probably of great historical importance.

I don't think so.

Then why have you not published them yet?

Because they were not important to me enough. I see no particular importance in them.

They are concerned with personal matters?
Well, partially. But I wouldn't care to publish them.

Well now. Can we move on to the time when you did eventually part company with Freud? It was partly, I think, with the publication of your book The Psychology of the Unconscious. *Is that correct?*

That was the real cause—I mean, the final cause, because it had a long preparation. You know, from the beginning, I had a reservation mentality. I couldn't agree with quite a number of his ideas.

Which ones in particular?

Well, chiefly his purely personal approach and his disregard of the historical conditions of man. You see, we depend largely upon our history. We are shaped through education, through the influence of the parents, which are by no means always personal. They were prejudiced or they were influenced by historical ideas or what I call 'dominance'. And that is a most decisive factor in psychology. We are not of today or of yesterday. We are of an immense age.

Was it not partly your clinical observation of psychotic cases which led you to differ from Freud on this?

It was partially my experience with schizophrenic patients that led me to the idea of certain general historical conditions.

Is there any one case that you can now look back on and feel that perhaps it was the turning point of your thought?

Oh, yes. I made quite a number of experiences of that sort, and I went even to Washington to study Negroes at the psychiatric clinic there in order to find out whether they have the same type of dreams as we have. And these experiences and others led me then to the hypothesis that there is an impersonal stratum in our psyche. And I can tell you an example.

We had a patient in the ward. He was quiet, but completely dissociated, schizophrenic. And he was in the clinic already for over twenty years. He had come into the clinic as a matter of fact as a young man, a little dark, and had no particular education. And once, I came into the ward, and he was obviously excited and called to me, took me by the lapel of my coat and led me to the window and said, "Doctor, now you must see, now look at it, look up at the sun and see how it moves. See, you must move your head too like this, and then you will see the follows of the sun. And, you know, that's the origin of the wind. And you see how the sun moves as you move your head from one side to the other."

Now, of course, I didn't understand it at all. I thought, Oh, there you are. He's just crazy. But that case remained in my mind. And four years later, I came across a paper written by the German historian, Dieterich, who had dealt with the so-called Mithras Liturgy, a part of the great Parisian Sorcerer Papyrus. And there he produced the part of the so-called Mithras Liturgy, namely it says there: "After the second prayer thou wilt see how the disc of the sun unfoldeth, and thou shalt see hanging down from it the tube, the origin of the wind; and when thou movest thy face to the regions of the East, it will move there. And if thou movest thy face to the region of the West, it will follow thee."

And instantly I knew, now *this* is it. This is the vision of my patient.

But how could you be sure that your patient wasn't unconsciously recalling something that somebody had told him?

Oh, no, quite out of question, because that thing was not known. It was in a magic papyrus in Paris, it wasn't even published. It was only published four years later, after I had observed it with my patient.

And this, you felt, proved that there was an unconscious which was something more than personal?

Oh, well, that was not a proof to me, but it was a hint. And I took the hint, yes.

Now, tell me, how did you first decide to start your work on the psychological types? Was that also as a result of some particular clinical experience?

Less so. It was a very personal reason, namely, to do justice to the psychology of Freud, also to that of Adler, and to find my own bearings. That helped me to understand why Freud developed such a theory; or why Adler developed his theory, his power principle.

Have you concluded what psychological type you are yourself?

Naturally, I have devoted a great deal of attention to that painful question, you know.

And reached a conclusion?

Well, you see, the type is nothing static. It changes in the course of life. But I most certainly was characterized by thinking. I always thought from early childhood on. And I had a great deal of intuition too. And I had a definite difficulty with feeling. And my relation to reality was not particularly brilliant. I was often at variance with the reality of things. Now, that gives you all the necessary data for the diagnosis.

During the 1930s, when you were working a lot with German patients, you did, I believe, forecast that a Second World War was very likely. Well now, looking at the world today, do you feel that a Third World War is likely?

I have no definite indications in that respect. But there are so many indications that one doesn't know what one sees—is it trees or is it wood? It's very difficult to say, because people's dreams contain apprehensions, you know. But it is very difficult to say whether they point to a war, because that idea is uppermost in people's minds. Formerly, you know, it has been much simpler. People didn't think of a war. And therefore, it was rather clear what the dreams meant. Nowadays, no more so. We are so full of apprehensions, fears, that one doesn't know exactly to what it points.

One thing is sure: a great change of our psychological attitude is imminent. That is certain.

Why?

Because we need more. We need more psychology. We need more understanding of human nature because the only real danger that exists is man himself. He is the great danger, and we are pitifully unaware of it. We know nothing of man, far too little. His psyche should be studied because we are the origin of all coming evil.

Well, does man, do you think, need to have the concept of sin and evil to live with? Is this part of our nature?

Well, obviously.

And of a redeemer?

That is an inevitable consequence.

This is not a concept which will disappear as we become more rational?

Well, I don't believe that man ever will deviate from the original pattern of his being. There will always be such ideas. For instance, if you do not directly believe in a personal redeemer, as it was the case with Hitler, or the hero worship in Russia, then it is an idea. It is a symbolic idea.

You have written, at one time or other, sentences which have surprised me a little about death. Now, in particular, I remember you said that death is psychologically just as important as birth; and, like it, it's an integral part of life. But surely it can't be like birth if it's an end, can it?

Yes, if it's an end. And there we are not quite certain about this end. Because, you know, there are these peculiar faculties of the psyche that it isn't entirely confined to space and time. You can have dreams or visions of the future. You can see around corners and such things. Only ignorance denies these facts. It's quite evident that they do exist and have existed always. Now, these facts show that the psyche, in part at least, is not dependent upon these confinements. And then what? When the psyche is not under that obligation to live in time and space alone—and obviously it doesn't—then to that extent the psyche is not submitted to those laws. And that means a practical continuation of life, of a sort of psychical existence beyond time and space.

Do you yourself believe that death is probably the end, or do you—?

I can't say. You see, the word 'believe' is a difficult thing for me. I don't *believe*. I must have a reason for a certain hypothesis. Either I know a thing, and when I know it, I don't need to believe it. I don't allow myself, for instance, to believe a thing just for the sake of believing it. I can't believe it. But when there are sufficient reasons for a certain hypothesis, I shall accept these reasons, naturally. I should say, we have to reckon with the possibility of so-and-so.

You've told us that we should regard death as being a goal, and that to shrink away from it is to evade life?

Yes, yes.

What advice would you give to people in their later life to enable them to do this, when most of them must, in fact, believe that death is the end of everything?

Well, you see, I have treated many old

people, and it's quite interesting to watch what the unconscious is doing with the fact that it is apparently threatened with the complete end: it disregards it. Life behaves as if it were going on. And so I think it is better for old people to live on, to look forward to the next day, as if he had to spend centuries. And then he lives properly. But when he is afraid, when he doesn't look forward, he looks back, he petrifies, he gets stiff, and he dies before his time. But when he is living on, look-ing forward to the great adventure that is ahead, then he lives. And that is about what the unconscious is intending to do. Of course, it's quite obvious that we are all going to die, and this is the sad finale of everything. But nevertheless there is something in us that doesn't believe it. Apparently, but this is merely a psycho-logical fact; it doesn't mean to me that it proves something; it is simply so. For in-stance, I may not know why we need salt, but we prefer to eat salt because you feel better. And so when you think in a certain way, you may feel considerably better. And I think if you think along the lines of nature, then you think properly.

And this leads me to the last question that I want to ask you. As the world becomes more technically efficient, it seems increasingly necessary for people to behave communally and collectively. Now, do you think it's possible that the highest development of man may be to submerge his own individuality in a kind of collective consciousness?

That's hardly possible. I think there will be a reaction. A reaction will set in against this communal dissociation. You know, man can't stand forever his nullification. Once there will be a reaction, and I see—I see it setting in, you know. When I think of my patients, they all seek their own existence, and to assure their existence against that complete atomization into nothingness or into meaninglessness. Man cannot stand a meaningless life.

ERIS

265 Riverside Dr.
New York, NY 10025

This transcript reproduces the full 1959 interview
between journalist John Freeman and Professor
Carl Gustav Jung, filmed at Jung's lakeside home
near Zurich for the BBC series *Face to Face*.

ISBN 978-1-967751-75-4

eris.press